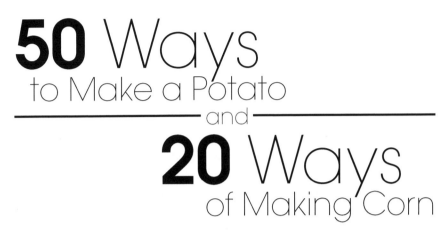

50 Ways
to Make a Potato
and
20 Ways
of Making Corn

2 in 1 Cook Book Plus Tips on Making Money

Sugar Diamond Princess Queen

Trafford rev.   11/08/2016

Trafford
PUBLISHING®   www.trafford.com
North America & international
toll-free: 1 888 232 4444 (USA & Canada)
fax: 812 355 4082

Potato Cake

Make to taste your own
Use Microwave, blender and oven if you desire.

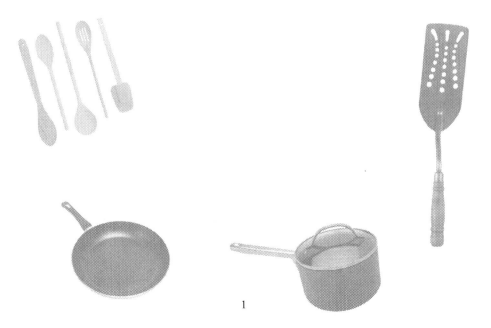

Potato Meal

Make to taste your own
Use Microwave, blender and oven if you desire.

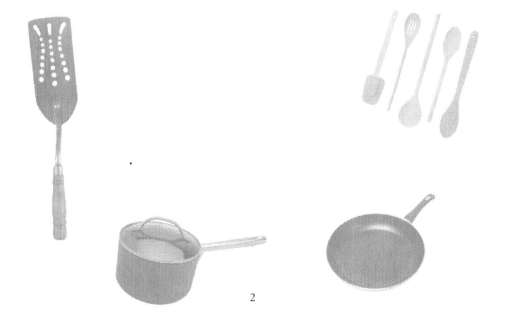

Baked Potatoes with Cheese

Make to taste your own
Use Microwave, blender and oven if you desire.

ℳashed ℙotato

Make to taste your own
Use Microwave, blender and oven if you desire.

Potato Salad

Make to taste your own
Use Microwave, blender and oven if you desire.

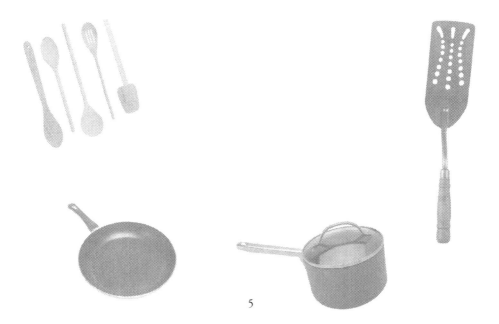

Potato Sandwich

Make to taste your own
Use Microwave, blender and oven if you desire.

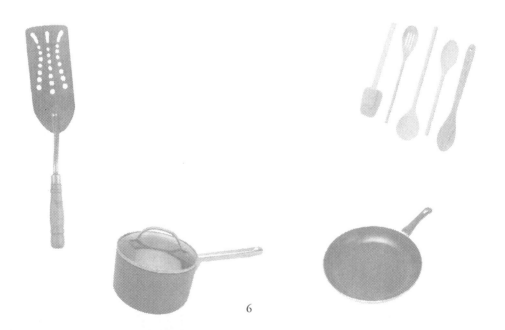

Potato Pie

Make to taste your own
Use Microwave, blender and oven if you desire.

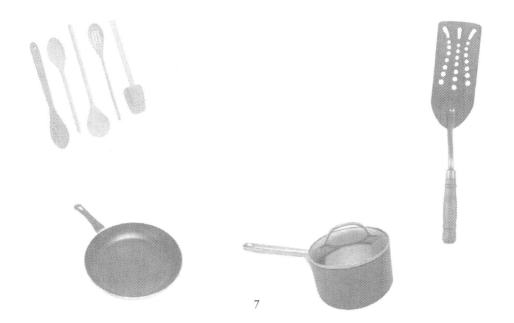

Potato Pizza

Make to taste your own
Use Microwave, blender and oven if you desire.

Potato Crepes

Make to taste your own
Use Microwave, blender and oven if you desire.

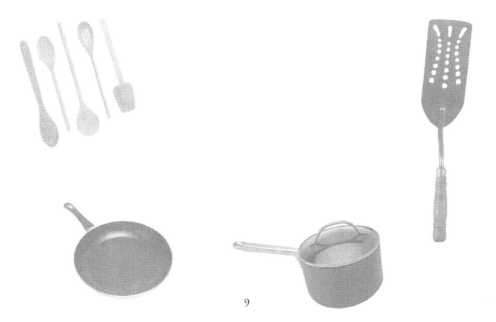

Potato Breakfast Bars

Make to taste your own
Use Microwave, blender and oven if you desire.

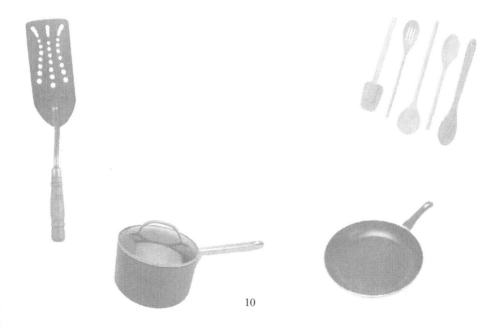

Potato Liquid Food

Make to taste your own
Use Microwave, blender and oven if you desire.

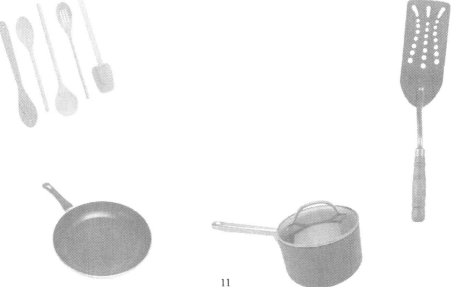

Egg and Potato

Make to taste your own
Use Microwave, blender and oven if you desire.

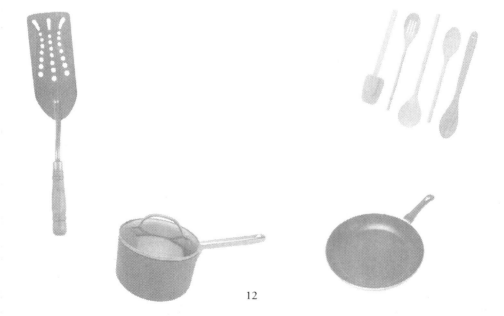

Potato Shells

Make to taste your own
Use Microwave, blender and oven if you desire.

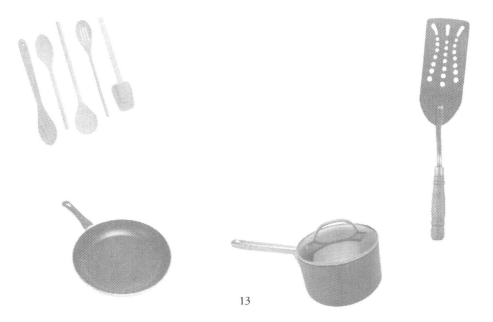

Potato Topping

Make to taste your own
Use Microwave, blender and oven if you desire.

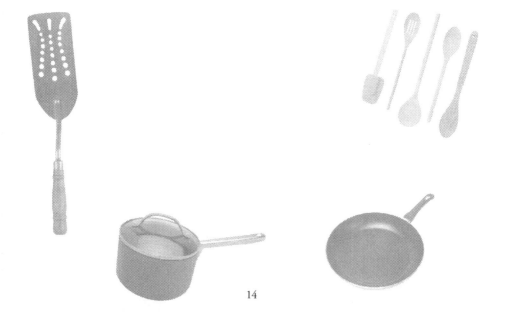

Potato Crepes

Make to taste your own
Use Microwave, blender and oven if you desire.

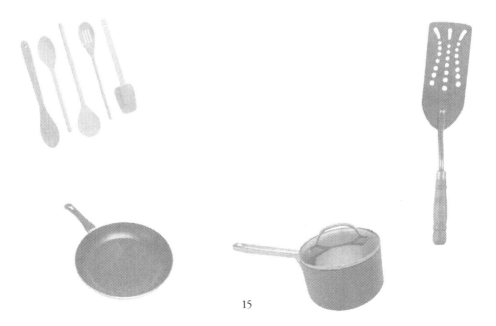

Mashed Potato

Make to taste your own
Use Microwave, blender and oven if you desire.

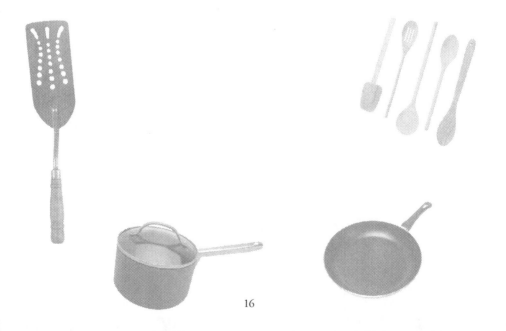

Potato Pancakes

Make to taste your own
Use Microwave, blender and oven if you desire.

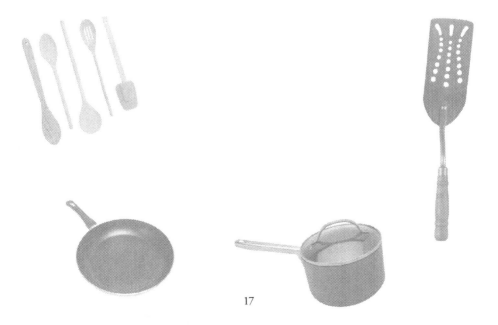

Potato Pancakes

Make to taste your own
Use Microwave, blender and oven if you desire.

Potato Chips

Make to taste your own
Use Microwave, blender and oven if you desire.

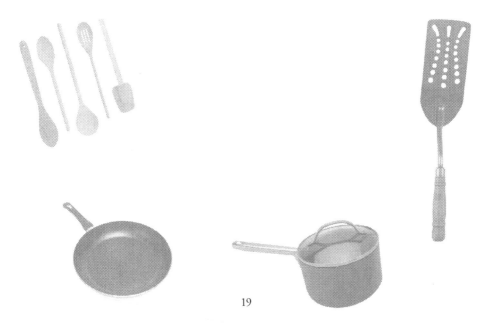

Potato Dips

Make to taste your own
Use Microwave, blender and oven if you desire.

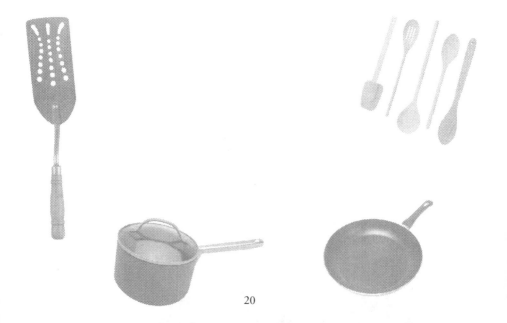

French Fries

Make to taste your own
Use Microwave, blender and oven if you desire.

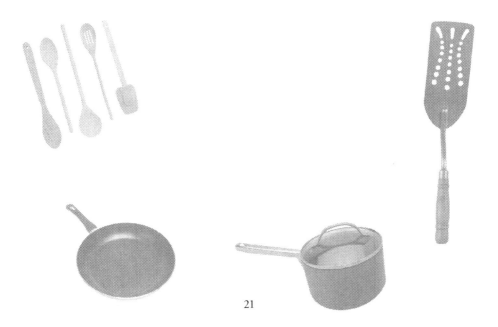

Cooked Potatoes with Skins

Make to taste your own
Use Microwave, blender and oven if you desire.

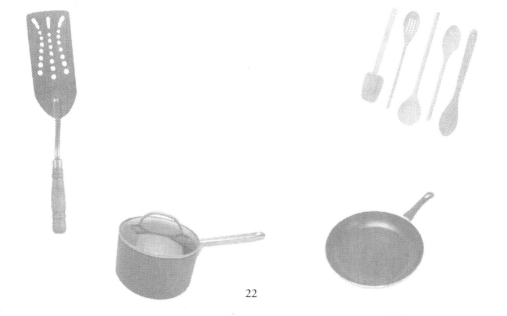

Boiled Potatoes

Make to taste your own
Use Microwave, blender and oven if you desire.

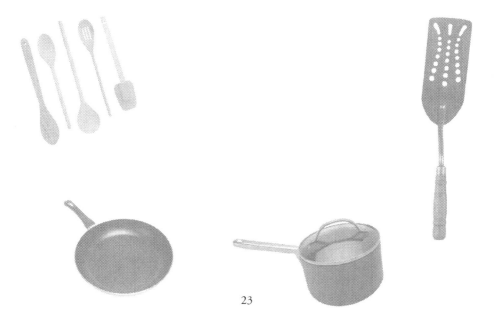

Crispy Potatoes

Make to taste your own
Use Microwave, blender and oven if you desire.

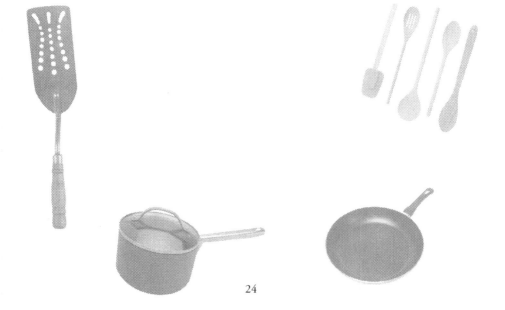

Whipped Potatoes

Make to taste your own
Use Microwave, blender and oven if you desire.

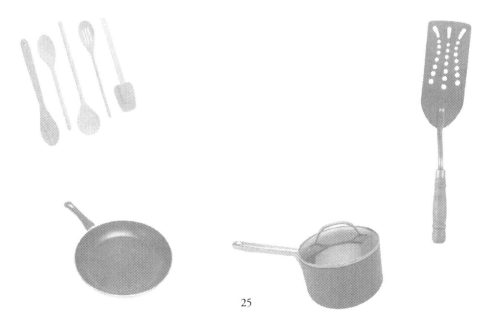

Potato Spread

Make to taste your own
Use Microwave, blender and oven if you desire.

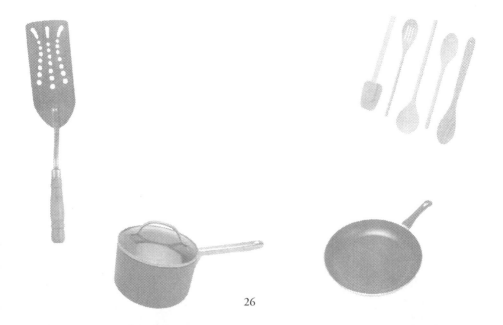

Onion Potato Snacks

Make to taste your own
Use Microwave, blender and oven if you desire.

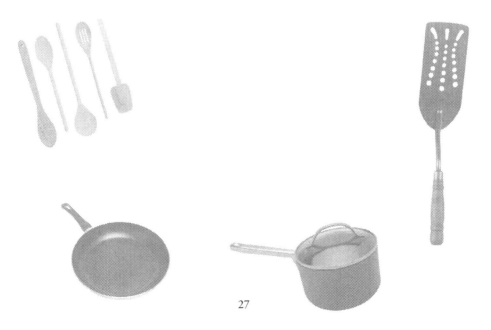

27

Steamed Potato

Make to taste your own
Use Microwave, blender and oven if you desire.

Potato Biscuit

Make to taste your own
Use Microwave, blender and oven if you desire.

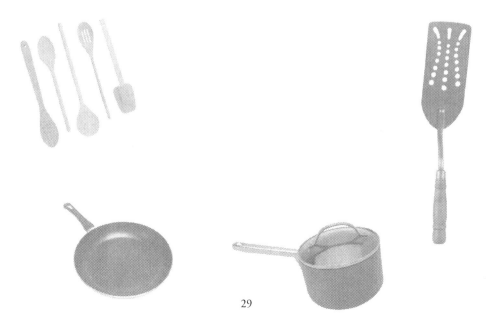

Potato Bread

Make to taste your own
Use Microwave, blender and oven if you desire.

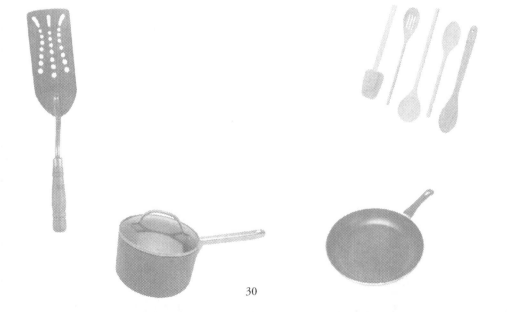

Potato Powder

Make to taste your own
Use Microwave, blender and oven if you desire.

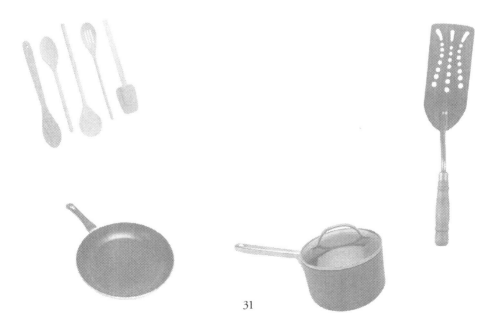

Potato Powder

Make to taste your own
Use Microwave, blender and oven if you desire.

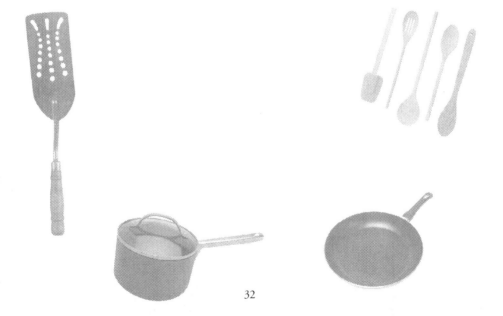

Potato Beans
(use smalls potatoes)

Make to taste your own
Use Microwave, blender and oven if you desire.

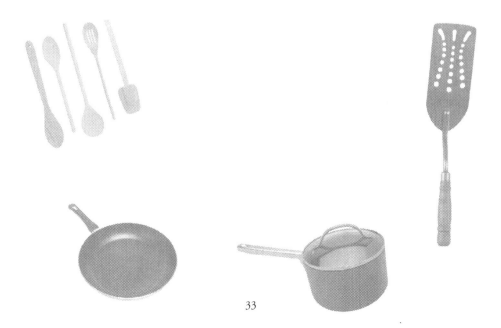

Potato and Peanut Butter

Make to taste your own
Use Microwave, blender and oven if you desire.

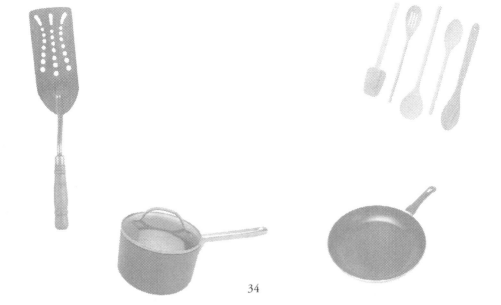

Barbeque Potatoes

Make to taste your own
Use Microwave, blender and oven if you desire.

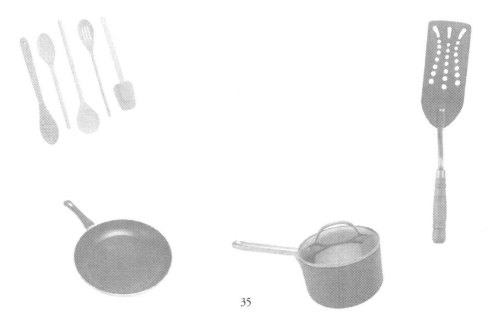

Potato Cookies

Make to taste your own
Use Microwave, blender and oven if you desire.

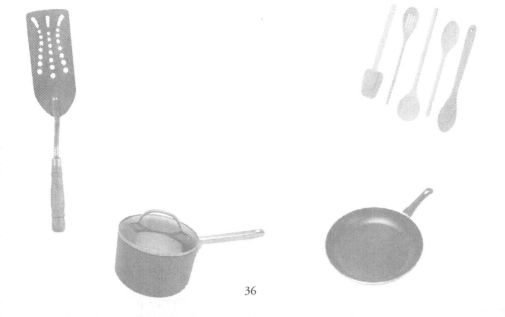

Creamy Magical Whipped Potatoes

Make to taste your own
Use Microwave, blender and oven if you desire.

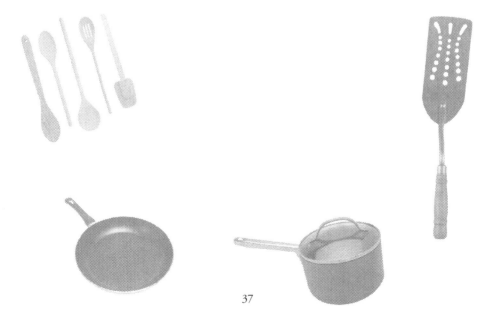

Potato Flakes

Make to taste your own
Use Microwave, blender and oven if you desire.

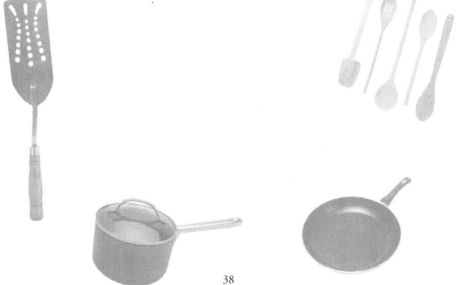

Potato Seasoning

Make to taste your own
Use Microwave, blender and oven if you desire.

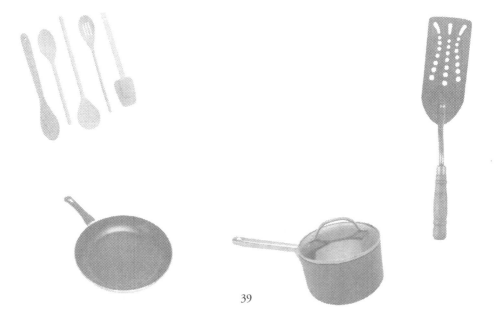

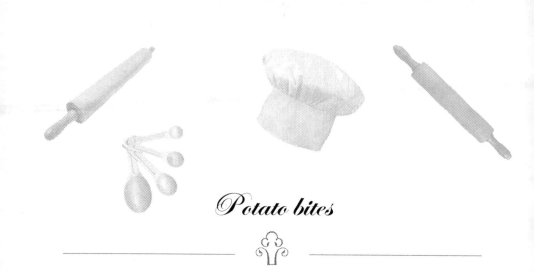

Potato bites

Make to taste your own
Use Microwave, blender and oven if you desire.

20 Ways to use Corn

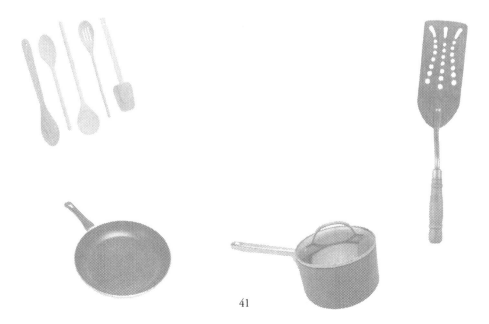

Corn Flour

Make to taste your own
Use Microwave, blender and oven if you desire.

Corn Stew

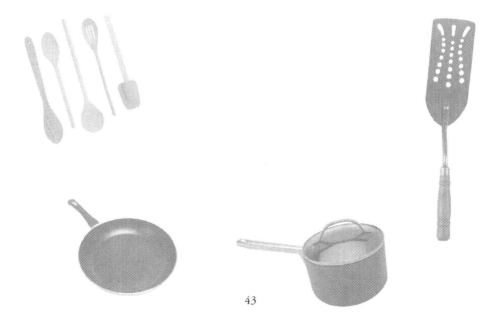

Corn Dog

Make to taste your own
Use Microwave, blender and oven if you desire.

Cooked Corn

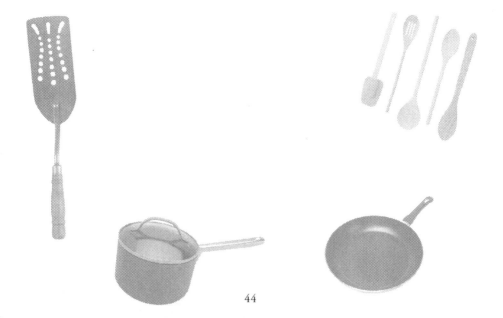

Corn Cake

Make to taste your own
Use Microwave, blender and oven if you desire.

Corn Pie

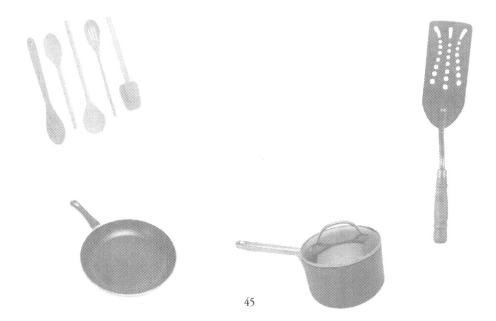

Corn Cereal

Make to taste your own
Use Microwave, blender and oven if you desire.

Corn Ears

Corn Meal

Make to taste your own
Use Microwave, blender and oven if you desire.

Corn Salad

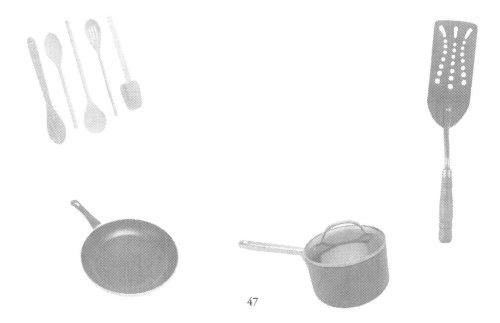

Fried Corn

Make to taste your own
Use Microwave, blender and oven if you desire.

Mashed Corn

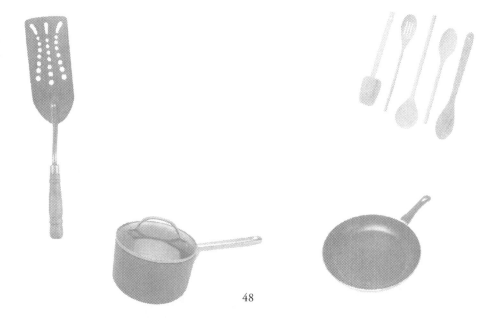

Corn and Potato

Make to taste your own
Use Microwave, blender and oven if you desire.

Corn and Rice

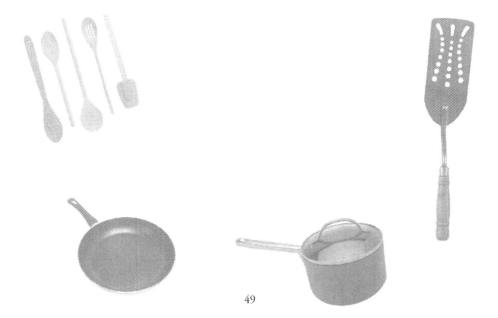

Corn Sauce

Make to taste your own
Use Microwave, blender and oven if you desire.

Corn Dough

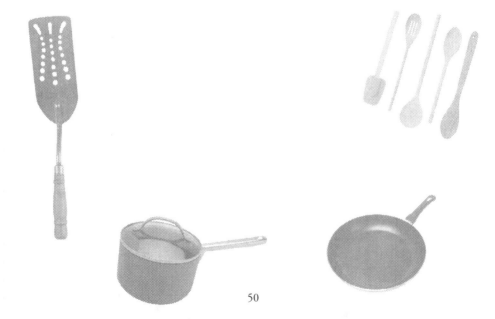

Tips To Make
Extra Money

1. Convert a hobby
2. Work part-time
3. Volunteer (sometimes they might help back or tip)
4. Become an extra actor or actress
5. Start a small farm
6. Join a union (sometimes it helps)

Thank you

This book is dedicated to the ones I love.